Reaching
UNSTOPPABLE
Self Confidence
for
Teens

The Ultimate Guide to Conquering fear with 3 minutes' exercises to Build self-Love and Manifest Your true potential.

By

Tracy Lowes

Copyright © 2024

All rights reserved.

No part of this publication may be reproduced, distributed, or transmitted in any form or by any means, including photocopying, recording, or other electronic or mechanical methods, without the prior written permission of the publisher, except in the case of brief quotations embodied in critical reviews and certain other noncommercial uses permitted by copyright law

TABLE OF CONTENTS

It is Possible……………………..1

The Hidden Power in You……..15

What is Self-Esteem?…………….25

What to do when Depressed?……...32

Conquer Your Biggest Fears……..41

The Ultimate Guide to Setting Goals..56

Mastering Your Emotions……...73

You Need A Dream………….85

Confidence Steps………….92

Exercises to Boost Self-Esteem…..111

1

It is Possible

A man wanted to climb a rough high mountain but did not know the right way to get there. He rested under an oak tree after trying so hard in the hot, scorching sun. After some time, he was jolted out of his sleep by the mouse of barking dogs. He staggered and was startled, but mustard was his last strength. He stood on his shaking, dry feet and headed towards the direction of the noise. Suddenly, he could see a man from a distance and, upon approaching him, asked for directions to the mountain. Do you know the way to the Sarmona mountains? Asked the traveler.

Just keep moving towards the left, and you will see a signpost. Follow its directions to get there. replied the hairy-skinned hunter.

The traveler left in a hurry as it was about to get dark. After walking for forty-five minutes, he approached the signpost; he could see the top of the mountain on the horizon. However, he was short of strength to continue. He sat near a rock and reached into his bag, hoping to get a bottle of water he thought would be left. When he brought out the bottle, it was empty.

He was surprised as he knew he left some quantity of water there. With a fainting knee and a body fast giving up on walking, he checked the bottle several times to find out why he could not get any water anymore. At this point, he discovered that his pen knife had pieced the bottles, so the remaining water must have poured out.

It seemed like all hope was lost, but he sat there staring at the mountain some distance away. And then this idea popped into his mind. He started remembering when he would go fishing with his parents. There was more water, and he would fill the little bag with fish at the end of each trip. These thoughts kept coming. It was a stream that had just begun to flow in his head. He started laughing, and by a stroke of luck, he regained some strength and completed his journey. Have you felt all alone although you are living with family members in the same house? Are you disconnected from everyone around you due to a low self-confidence about yourself? Let's learn from this story.

Let's see some causes of loneliness;

- *Choices you have made in life,*
- *Moving to a new apartment*
- *A serious health condition that may render one to be isolated.*

- *The loss of a loved one*
- *Depression And*
- *low self-esteem.*

Have you been going through a difficult face of life where you are lonely? It is usually a passing phase. Do not allow such a moment to take away your joy. According to medical experts, loneliness might cause cognitive decline and other psychiatric issues.

A recent study, shows that self-confidence exercises such as wring, shading and ticking your moods and a given time can help reduce such emotional anxiety.

Speak out.

Now after making some phone calls and you see that no one responds, do not feel conquered. Just keep trying. You may engage in a healthy coping strategy that allows you to feel better. Drawing, knitting, or gardening are a few examples of solitary activities that help you healthily deal with your loneliness.

What you can do

Reach out to old friends. This may not be the best idea, but we are trying to give you a chance. Every step counts.

Old friends are easier to talk with than new friends. When you reach out to them, the worst-case scenario is for them to tell you they are busy.

Yes, it might not always go the way we plan. That's totally fine.

And what if they answered in the affirmative? That will be an opportunity to reach out and reconnect. You can watch films, play, or recall past events which you have been together. This is better than feeling alone.

For example, your classmates, friends from the same neighborhood, or members of the same sports club are all people you already share a lot in common. From this meeting, you can choose to continue or seek for another.

Now, if you are really shy, you can begin with a text. A simple message saying hello and stating the reason fr the message might be enough to spark an interest

Connect more.

Some of your efforts should be geared toward making new friends. Check your local directory. There are many volunteer groups and community services that might be nearby. A visit to these places might spark your interest in meeting new people. If you are like me and you love to help out, then find non-governmental organizations that have goals you can connect with. Attending various events helps you associate with more people.

Read more

You are reading one now. What happens when you are done? Yes, you are right. You can read another book. Some of our books have exercises which you can complete in them. This method has a twofold advantage. It connects you to other characters in It, and you are gaining valuable knowledge.

Go on YouTube

The internet might be a good place to hang out and be connected with our families. You will meet people across the world.

YouTube is a great place to be entertained and many tutorials are free to learn. Many teens also use Tiktok. Tiktok is good when used correctly. I spend less time there. What's most important is snapping out of depression or loneliness.

The truth is entertainment through videos can help with loneliness, but it's never a permanent solution. So keep in mind that you need always to go back and watch more videos to overcome your lonely moments.

Learn More

Skills can be gotten from what we are taught in classroom though an experienced teacher We can learn online by taking an online course or a lesson. After this lesson, our minds and brains are stimulated with visuals. Then we start putting everything that we have learned together.

This process is important and one you should take with rapt attention.

For example, you can Sign up for a karate class or learn the piano.

What are your hobbies?

Can you sing, do journaling, cook a good m,eal always?

Loneliness is taken care of by doing the things you love. You can take the initiative to learn a skill.

If you don't have any hobbies, make it a priority to find one. Experiment with different activities, from fishing to pottery, until you discover things that you love.

Be kind

Whatever you want, give it to someone, and you will get it back. Do you want to be loved, understood, appreciated, or celebrated? You can be kind to a soul out there. Have you understood that "whatsoever a man sows…"?

This verse says it all. We all have our wants, our desires but we do not feel compelled to do for others. You don't owe anyone anything. Just obeying what it says is enough for great forces in the universe to be released for your good.

Support a small business owner.

Spend time with your grandparents.

Acts of kindness you can follow.

Give a care package for a homeless person.

Donate food, toys, books, and so much more.

2

The Hidden Power in You

There is a hidden power within which you can exploit. You were made a complete being. Eating, drinking, sleeping, running, and jumping, does not change what you are. I went to visit my friends village in Vienna. It was a remote area with tall trees. There were lots of grasses there. While driving along, I sent him a message that I wanted to stop over at his local village. In a few minutes, the reply came. 'You are welcome.' He said. I drove for thirty-five minutes more until I saw the signpost showing that I was in his village. On getting there, I parked beside a popular restaurant to eat some food as I had not eaten in a while before embarking on this journey.

When I got there, I kept my bag and requested a local dish, it dawned on me that I had some time left as Anthony wouldn't be available until the next 2 hours. He works as a security officer and is only free in the evenings.

Thinking of what to do with the time, I went to his house and waited for thirty minutes before his arrival.

Reaching his house, I entered headed straight to the sitting room. Just then, his kids saw me and alerted his wife that they had a visitor.

After greetings, I told her I would wait till he returns from work.
Sitting in an old, dusty but strong chair which was what I could find there. After a while, saw a little ant moving all around near the wall. It was a worker trying to lift a tiny bit of bread size. It kept on trying to move it towards a direction in which lots of household items were blocked. Despite the obstacles, the ant kept on

trying, and each time it got hold of the food, it fell off before he could arrive at his destination.

I kept asking why it can't give up? It's too tiny to carry both the tiny size of bread and its body weight. I was wrong, though, as it took 20 minutes to get it done. He wanted to climb the barriers made up of cartons, shoes, and electronic gadgets.

You can do better. You are stronger than this ant. There is a hidden power that lies within you.

When you develop this hidden potential, you will reach unimaginable heights.

It's just like planting a seed of grain. When it's well-watered, then it starts to grow and sprout beyond our initial efforts.

After a while, you will have a healthy plant-bearing fruit and ready for harvest.

Our Thoughts are like seeds sown into our minds. They can grow and become powerful when we put our attention and focus on them.

> Hold a picture of yourself long and steadily enough in your mind's eye, and you will be drawn toward it.
>
> — Napoleon Hill

Your thoughts become intense when there is focus, passion and dedication to fulfill a particular thought and make it part of your experience and existence which makes all the difference.

Therefore, every thought that comes to your mind might affect a few or more persons. That's the reason why a worthy goal affects everyone around you.

For example, when Mr. Stan decided to buy a house the same year he got married, he never knew this would impact his wife, his work, and his bank.

It took him six months to get the foundation done by the building engineer. On one occasion, after checking out the building construction, he got home and met his wife crying. Sensing that something was off, he joined her in to cry. Later that evening, she started telling him the reason she was crying. It was because she said she missed her antenatal classes. Mr. Stan was so tired that he didn't know what to do. It was his first year of living as a family, and he had lots of projects to complete. That's what goal setting does to you. Many are going to be influenced by it.

You will attract many other people who can help you in reaching those goals.

How **Can you really tap into this creative power of**

> **Whatever we plant in our subconscious mind and nourish with repetition and emotion will one day become a reality.**
>
> Earl Nightingale

your mind to reach your goals?

You can visualize your thoughts.

> Visualize the end, and start at the beginning.
> Carolyn Brown

Your imagination is a powerful tool and a good mind activity to reach any goals you set.

You can go ahead and observe with detail as a

> When you combine powerful visualizations with deliberate actions, you can have whatever you seek.
> ~ Whitney Gordon-Mead

scientist would. For example, if you wanted to draw a chameleon with the information you have learned about your mind and the hidden power in you, add more coloring and background information to it.

Do this activity consistently, and Your subconscious mind will take them to be your new reality.

Just as you have seen it in the movies over again. The Actions and events, along with the emotions you meditate on, will manifest on your way.

It might take some time but that's how nature works. Nothing happens. Start with the thought and then the actions and planning. Put more effort in planning and carrying out the plan.

This is how you change negative habits and establish new habits or skills.

Always check your thoughts. Guard against anything that might prompt you to say, 'it's time to end it all'. Remember Thomas Edison. How many times he failed before he became successful with the light bulb.

You've should keep trying, as you may succeed, or you may not succeed.

Do not wish yourself to fail even when things don't work out the way you plan them. Go ahead and plan it anyway.

Stay motivated all day. Let your mind think good thoughts that bring good, happy, and positive results.
Your Thoughts Become Your Reality
You can try any of this:

Your thoughts define and affect your life.

3

What is Self-Esteem?

Self-esteem is to how we see and judge ourselves. It's the opinion we have about our own self-worth. We all have some level of self-esteem since we develop ideas of who we are based on different life events. Things that impacts your self-esteem include:

- How we were raised
- Our education
- Our relationships with friends and family
- Where we live
- What we believe in

- Our general outlook on life
- Our strengths and weaknesses

Your self-esteem changes with time. Many has been living with low self confidence.

A low self-esteem makes you focus more on your faults. You might feel unsuccessful, unattractive, or unlovable and easily hurt by others. Don't let negative judgments, mistakes, disagreements, or "failures" get to you.

Alice's Story of Low Self-Esteem

As a teenager, I constantly felt anxious about everything and had trouble opening up. I was insecure and struggled whenever I left my comfort zone. At university, my anxiety got much worse. I over-analyzed things, was very insecure in relationships, and developed low body image. I wouldn't let anyone see me without lots of makeup. I became paranoid that people disliked me.

When I finally saw a doctor, he diagnosed me with low self-esteem. I realized he was right, though I had ignored the signs because I was naive.

In most relationships, I've felt insecure, believing I wasn't good enough. I saw myself as boring so I had trouble making friends or going on dates.

My self-judgments were always negatively biased because I never saw anything positive in myself. Healthy self-esteem is important for being your best self and reducing anxiety. After improving my self-image, I could finally process things rationally, make decisions more easily, and complete my education with a positive attitude.

Our upbringing plays a big role in developing self-esteem. How we were treated, who we spent time with, and what friends we had impacts our mindset and shapes our identity. Certain childhood experiences can lead to either high or low self-worth.

What Does It Mean to Have A High Self-Esteem?

- Feeling listened to
- Receiving praise
- Getting attention
- Feeling loved
- Having good friends
- Succeeding in school or sports

- Being respected

Having opportunities to participate in activities

What Is The Meaning Of Low Self-Esteem?

- Facing constant criticism
- Feeling ignored, neglected, or abused
- Being bullied or made fun of
- Believing imperfections are weaknesses
- Struggling in school or sports
- Feeling different from peers
- Living in an unsupportive environment

While the past matters, adulthood events also impact self-esteem. Other factors include:

- Harsh or excessive criticism

- Feeling like an outsider at work or elsewhere

- Abuse - physical, emotional, or sexual
- Appearance concerns
- Financial stress
- Job-related stress or unemployment
- Family/friend/partner relationship issues
- Divorce or separation
- Trauma from accidents, assault, grief, etc.
- Health problems or illness

4

What to do when Depressed?

From the 2019 statistics reported by the center for disease control (CDC) about the mental health conditions of young people, it is estimated that about 1 in 3 teens had experienced feelings of hopelessness or sadness, and roughly 1 in 6 had reported having suicide tendencies in the past year alone.

Teens have had to undergo so much life challenges ranging from bullying, peer pressures, family and school stress. All these are taking place alongside the growing up and body changes they are going through. These can cause emotional stress which might lead to depression or other health issues.

Although some of these can be handled with care, you need to be mindful of your mental state every day.

In all these things, you are not alone. There are many teens out there who have stood strong and become individuals that exceled at their jobs and life pursuit. This is what this book is all about, to tell you you can be different. We understood the pressure and how bad things can really get so quickly. Hold on and it will be worth it.

Do what you love.

What do you love to do I your spare time? Do you play an instrument? Do you read books and consume literature? Do you play games? Do you love to cook? It time to do whatever that will make you happy. Do not be afraid of what people will say. Remember that people will keep talking about people and places. Let them keep talking about you. You never know if this is the motivation you need.

Write about how you feel.

It's a free world and you need to take advantage of that. We might not all be good speakers. We can write as well. You can write about anything and deliver it to those that need to read it. You are freeing up your mind from so much pressure. Expressing your thought is an activity that the brain loves.

Be kind

Do not hurt you. You are important to nature and to your family. There is a role you have come to play and you don't want to hurt your chances. remind yourself that you can do anything you set your mind to do. Sometimes, we are beating down by failures. They are also part of life. Every successful man out there has experience failure.

Feeling worthless could signal a low self-esteem. It can make you feel:

- You are not smart or talented enough
- Worried about what others think
- Like you can't do things

- Embarrassed about how you look
- Blame yourself for things
- Obsessed with mistakes

Hair Problem

- Managing my hair was a big deal for me as I hated it. Growing up was a bit different as most of my family members had a straight hair. Mine was different and it got everyone in my family confused on how to help me with it.

- After washing and brushing it, I will leave it that way without remembering if I ever combed it. Using some curl mousse, cream, or gel, that I would have totally manageable spirals instead of barely tamed frizz.

My stepmom made me feel unwanted. She made fun of me needing help and turned my half-siblings against me. My brother once tried to hit me with a toy truck when I didn't want to move. My 8-year-old sister also mocks me. I've learned to forgive them. Showing myself empathy is hard though. I'm not fully over it but I'm better than I was.

I pretend to be happy and outgoing so kids will like me. Now I have friends but we're not close. No one knows the real me or my interests. I hoped a girl would like me back but the only one who pays attention tries touching me in weird ways. She's my friend but talks about other guys. Does that mean something is wrong with me? I exercise, have hobbies, and try improving my anxiety but I feel empty inside around others. Please help - I don't want to wait until after school ends. My mental health is declining.

What I can do when I'm depressed

5

Conquer Your Biggest Fears

Are you worried about life after school or graduation? Due to past failure as humans, we are quite nervous about the future.

Instead worry about your test scores, or a broken relationship, look beyond the what's happening today. We have different colleges you can study. You need to know which college will accept you.

What if you have successfully gained admission into college but your performance have been a source of concern. You are not alone. We actually do worry for a good cause. You don't have to do your work alone.

Try finding out what you need. You need to conquer your greatest fear by proper and honest assessment. So what do you need to do to reach your goals?

Starting a job and messing up

Your first day at a full time job might not be the best day of all. Give yourself some time. As with everything, you will get better at it.

Picking the wrong career

No one wants to be in a wrong career but it happens. The problem becomes complicated when the individual discovers it very late. He will feel cheated and believe that he has wasted so much time doing what he doesn't want to do in life. Such scenario can be avoiding if you

can follow what you love. There are so much choices you can make with the options you have today.

A simple career guidance will come in handy.

Making New friends

Making new friends is often part of starting the next chapter in life. That can be tough. But the new people you meet at work or college will have a lot in common with you.

It's not easy leave your friends and find new ones. Finding others who like the same stuff as you can help you make friends. Getting used to living with roommates or in a dorm can be tricky too. If you want to make a list of your favorite activities, I can help you find places where those people hang out.

Fear of Failing

Daily pressure are caused by

1. Going to college

2. Getting a "good" job

3. Living a "good" life

4. Getting good grades

When your life is on the line, you'll be scared of "messing up."

Fear of Letting Others Down

Many don't want to disappoint their parents. They don't want to be seen as "bad friends." They want to be someone other than the teammate who misses the winning shot. This can be bad if it goes too far. Some may try to make others happy instead of finding confidence in themselves.

Fear of Rejection

Many are afraid of being rejected by friends. We love to be accepted but have we considered the price we have to pay ?

FEELING EMBARRASED

In a world where social status means everything for teens, humiliation or anything threatening their reputation is scary. If you make one mistake, you could end up in a viral video. Saying the wrong thing could make the popular kids not like you. If you embarrass yourself on a date, you may never get another one. Teens fear embarrassment when the stakes feel so high, even though no one likes feeling humiliated.

Show that you care

When you empathize, you make a real, deep connection with your teen. You're helping them feel understood, that you take their problem seriously, and that you care. You have to "be with them" emotionally. When they feel less alone, they feel less afraid.

Encourage Communication

No relationship can exist without communication, whether between parents and their teens or anyone else. Most people stop communicating as well during the teen years.

But keep the lines open so your teen feels safe coming to you about anything. Talking about your own experiences can help them feel comfortable opening up too. That way, they feel okay sharing their thoughts and feelings.

My three teen kids can look back on stuff I did and what happened because of it. As they deal with similar things, knowing Dad has been there and can give advice is helpful.

Grow up

Use failure as a chance to grow, not a sign someone "made the wrong choice." Failure is the flipside of success.

Anxiety can be a Good thing

If humans had no fear at all, our species probably wouldn't exist anymore. Fear can be helpful sometimes. It might stop a teen from cheating on a test, walking along a cliff's edge, or experimenting with drugs. Teens need to know to respect their scared feelings instead of ignoring them or talking themselves out of it.

But fear can also be bad. It's probably unhealthy for a teen to be so anxious that it stops them from normal activities, controls their behavior, or puts too much pressure on them. So it's important to address.

Don't Criticize

An adult might think it's "silly" for a teen to fear losing a friend or missing a weekend activity. But if it matters to the teen, it should matter to the adult too.

Don't dismiss your teen's worries as dumb, baseless, or unjustified.

Listen with empathy.

Your teen deserves that safe space.

Teach and Model Critical Thinking

Fears come from thoughts and ideas. You can better manage your fears if you can change what you believe. With new ideas, you can often get rid of fear and doubt.

If you teach teens how to build healthy, productive thoughts, they can overcome fear from the inside out. But this will benefit them as adults too.

Tools like the Egg Model and positive affirmations can be very powerful for teens. Introduce them to these concepts and work together to apply them in your lives. In the end, your own example is your strongest teaching tool.

Helpful Tips

Be a positive: things might not be perfect, give it your all.

Enjoy yourself: play and have fun after school or when you are done with your exam.

Change negative thoughts: Challenge beliefs that make you feel bad, like thinking you'll fail.

Use test-taking strategies:

1. When you get the exam, write down important information you're worried about forgetting on the back of the paper.

2. allocate enough time you can to each question.

3. focus on what you know. Understand the type of questions you have. Is it a multiple-choice or a True/False questions, these are clues for other answers.

4. breathe deeply, then take a break

If you find out you are getting worried, stop and break free from such thinking pattern.

· Go on a 30-second break.

· Focus on something specific around you, like the sound of the room's lights buzzing, to clear your mind.

· Pay attention to your physical sensations caused by anxiety. Sometimes, when you fully experience them, they can go away.

6

The Ultimate Guide to Setting Goals

Last summer, I thought about what fun things my kids could do over the 9-week break from school. My son wanted to get better at playing soccer. So I told him that if he practiced kicking the soccer ball 10,000 times, he would get really good, while other kids just sat around looking at screens.

I made a worksheet to help the kids pick summer goals. We had so much fun that the whole family did it! We filled out the worksheets, put them up on the wall, and helped each other work on our goals. I even used it to lose weight, learn guitar, and learn new songs.

The worksheet guided us in setting goals and making plans to reach them. Instead of just wasting time on the internet, I wanted the kids to focus for weeks on getting good at something. That way they feel proud of what they accomplished.

Since school is off this week, the kids asked to do the worksheets again. So I got them out and explained how it works.

Just thinking of a goal in your head doesn't count. You have to write down your goals. For example, "lose weight" isn't a good goal. A better goal is something like "eat 1500 calories each day and exercise twice a week for 30 minutes."

The goal should be a new habit that leads to the result you want. That's the only way to make the change last.

Then write down why you want to reach that goal. For example: **The things I love about me is**

Thing I Do Without Getting Tired

You can choose to set a good example of being healthy for your little brother or sister.

IF YOU WANT TO LIVE A HAPPY LIFE, TIE IT TO A GOAL, NOT TO PEOPLE OR THINGS.

—Albert Einstein

Goals I would love to reach this year /month

Sometimes you'll keep at it because you feel really motivated. Sometimes you'll keep at it because the steps are super easy. Make sure you always have both! Just because the steps are easy doesn't mean you should forget why the goal matters. But just because you feel motivated doesn't mean you should make the steps too hard.

This worksheet focuses on why we wanted our goals and the small steps to take each week. For example, I used it to change my diet from eating pizza and soda almost every day to following a strict healthy diet. The changes were so gradual I barely noticed. Eating healthy just became my new normal. And I didn't even miss the pizza and soda.

Just work on increasing the study times to thrice per hour, taking 10 minute breaks. You can always change it later.

Also, set up rewards you can give yourself when you reach a step. Like if your first goal is to study 10 minutes, let yourself play a game on your phone when you're done. But never play the game unless you did the study goal for that day. Choose something you really want for your reward. And only allow the reward if you reach that day's goal.

Then when you reach your big overall goal that you first wrote down, give yourself an awesome reward to celebrate! Over time, setting goals and rewards just becomes a normal rhythm. This method makes it easy because you adjust bit-by-bit over time. You don't have to take on too many goals at once either. Start with just one goal, work on it for 2 months. Then add another goal for 2 months. Then 2 goals together for 2 months. And so on.

If you dare to dream big and set goals, you can achieve amazing things!

Here is an attempt to rewrite the text providing goal setting examples for a 10-year-old audience:

Setting goals can help you achieve amazing things! Let's go through an example.

First, write down all the areas where you'd like to improve or achieve something. For me, I wrote down:

Spiritual (feeling peaceful, having purpose)

Emotional (feeling confident, being nice to others)

Physical (getting healthier, being better at sports)

Mental (getting smarter, learning new things)

Social (making friends, being a good friend)

Creative (writing stories, drawing, making crafts)

GOALS I WANT TO REACH!

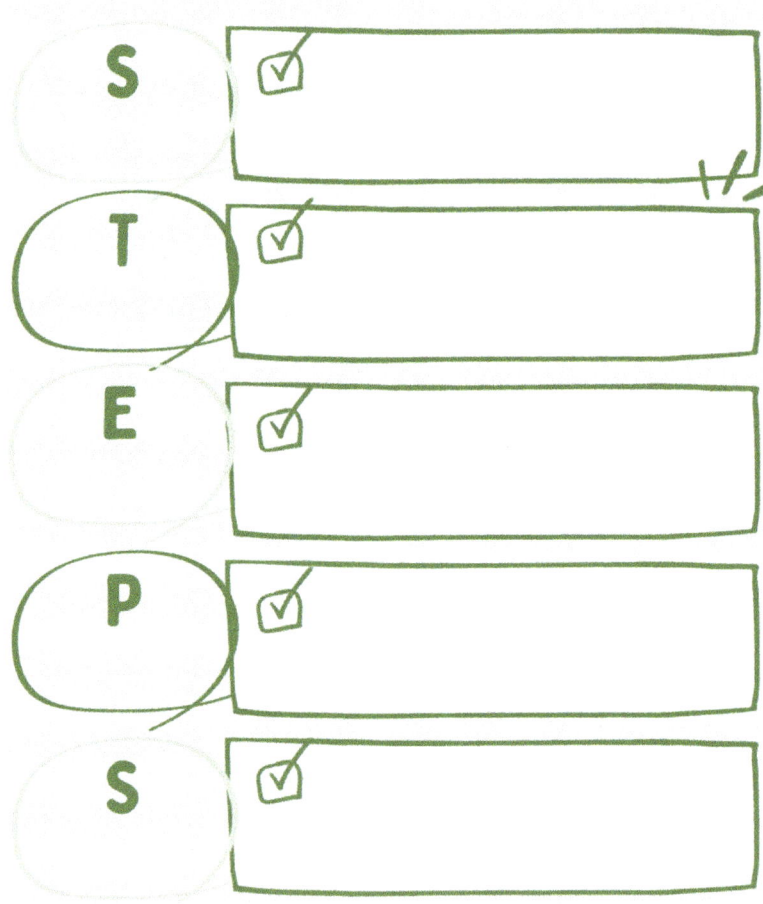

- **S**
- **T**
- **E**
- **P**
- **S**

List and arrange them according to the most important.

Here's an example:

Year 1 goals:

Get better at soccer (physical)

Make 2 new friends (social)

Year 2 goals:

Feel more confident (emotional)

Learn to draw animals (creative)

Year 3 goal:

Get all A's in school (mental)

See? Just pick 3 big goals per year.

Then for each big goal, write down smaller goals that will help you get there. Like for my soccer goal:

- Practice kicking 10 minutes every day

- Do footwork drills before each game

- Watch videos to learn new moves

Setting smaller goals is like giving yourself a step-by-step way to get better at something!

Be really focused this year. A goal you have set helps you do just that. Dare to dream big!

Draw Your Biggest Accomplishment

7

Mastering Your Emotions

Big feelings are just part of growing up. When you're a pre-teen or teenager, you might notice your mood change a lot. One day you feel super happy and excited. The next day you feel bored, grumpy or sad. You also probably want more alone time than you used to.

These emotional ups and downs happen because your body and brain are going through big changes. Here are some reasons why:

Body changes. Your body is changing a lot right now. You might feel embarrassed or want more privacy. Or if you're developing earlier or later than your friends, you might have complicated feelings. Also, just not getting enough sleep or food can make your mood drop. Enough sleep and exercise helps manage feelings.

Brain changes. Your brain is changing too! New chemicals make your body mature. They also give you new or intense romantic and sexual feelings that can be confusing. Also, your brain doesn't finish developing until your early 20s. So it's still learning to control strong feelings. That's why little things might set off big emotional reactions.

Life changes. You have more responsibilities now, like school, friends, and family. You're figuring out how to handle problems yourself instead of going to parents. All these thoughts and challenges affect your moods. Big family issues do too.

These emotional highs and lows are practice for learning to deal with grownup feelings. Your parents and trusted adults can help guide you. Over time and with their support, you'll get better at understanding yourself and managing mood swings as you grow up. The teen years have lots of changes, but you've got this!

When you get super angry or sad or scared, it might feel like you're going to explode! You might try stuffing those feelings down deep inside so you don't have to deal with them. But that usually doesn't work very well or very long.

Trying hard to hide big feelings takes a lot of work. It's like trying to hold a beach ball under the water – you might be able to do it for a little bit, but eventually you get tired and the feelings "pop up" anyway. Then things usually get messy!

What if there was a better way? Instead of hiding feelings or pretending they're not there, you could practice letting them out in helpful ways. This is called "self-regulation."

Self-regulation means finding good ways to express feelings and handle challenges. This is way better than self-control, which is just forcing yourself to bottle things up inside. Tis method ensures your feelings are taken into consideration.

It helps you reject unlawful peer pressure to do something bad. You can say no but then feel guilty, worried, angry, left out of the "fun." Those feelings build up pressure inside.

With self-regulation, you could still say no to shoplifting. But you could also tell your friend afterwards why you felt uncomfortable and check that your friendship is okay. Letting those feelings out helps deflate them, like letting air out of a balloon.

Being able to understand and express feelings helps you handle tough situations. Big, intense emotions are part of life – they happen to everyone sometimes!

You can grow up to be caring, responsible, happy, and successful personality! But some parents expect kids to control feelings all by themselves. It's important to know that managing feelings takes time and practice. It's not always easy! Kids need help and guidance with this while they learn. Like how plants need the right amount of sun, water and soil to grow strong, kids need the right things to build emotional control.

Here is what kids your age need to grow emotionally healthy:

1. Parents who calmly talk about and understand your feelings. This helps you recognize emotions.

2. A safe space at home where you can share feelings without getting in trouble.

3. Rules that fit your age to help you make good choices.

4. Parents who show you how to express feelings positively.

5. Gentle tips on how to share feelings appropriately.

6. Learning how your actions impact others.

But parents can only provide these things if they manage their own feelings first, before reacting to your behavior. They need to stay calm, remember they love you, and respond with care. However, parents must also work on being aware of their own emotions to do this well.

Kids get better at controlling their emotions by seeing parents express caring feelings and firmly enforce rules. The best thing parents can do is take care of their own emotional health. This means admitting they aren't perfect! When parents make mistakes, they should apologize and fix them, just like they want you to.

When parents work on feeling their best, they model good behavior for you.

How You Feel

Let's take 20 minutes to explore your emotions!

1. Name your feeling. Look at the Feeling Words page. We all have different emotions. Can you pick one you felt today or yesterday? It takes practice to know what you feel inside. As I close my eyes placing my hands on my heart, I can find the right word. Try it! Once you know the feeling, write it in the heart of your Feeling Buddy worksheet.
2. Draw your emotional face. Show the feeling you picked by drawing a face on your Feeling Buddy. Did your face match the emotion?
3. Rate your emotion. To show how strongly you felt it, write a number 1-4 on your Feeling Buddy's left hand. 1 is a little and 4 is a lot!
4. Tell someone you trust. Think of someone you can talk to about this feeling. Write their name on

your Feeling Buddy's right hand. Stuffed animals work too! Sharing helps us feel better.
5. Respond kindly. You can choose how to react to feelings. Did you know? It's good to respond in a caring way to yourself and others. Draw or write your healthy idea.

Responsible Actions

For 10 minutes, let's learn to pick wise responses to emotions. This will help you in social settings.

A. Thumbs Up/Thumbs Down Game

I'll read statements. Show thumbs up if it's responsible. Thumbs down if it's not.

- Yelling at my brother makes me feel better when angry.
- Bouncing a ball makes me feel better when sad.
- Hugging my stuffed bunny makes me feel better when bored.
- Listening to music makes me feel better when tired.

- Picking on someone makes me feel better when mad.
- Criticizing others makes me feel better when jealous.
- Playing with my hamster makes me feel better when lonely.

B. Fill out your Responsible Actions worksheet (just for you).

A Good Thing That Happened Toda**y**

1

What Compliment Should I Give Myself Today

2

THE BEST PART OF TODAY WAS

8

You Need A Dream

Dreams are your brain's way of being creativity while you sleep. Some will make you smile; others will worry you. Paying attention to all your dreams can unlock ideas and hidden messages from your own mind!
What Should You Do With Your Dreams? When you wake up from a really exciting or interesting dream, try writing it down or drawing pictures of what happened. This can be lots of fun and let you explore your dreams

more. Tell your family about dreams that made strong feelings happen - either good ones or bad ones. Talking about them can help you understand them better. Before bed, you can even tell yourself "I want to have a dream about. .." and see if it happens! This lets you pick what you dream about.

What could you do in your imagination? Dream BIG Goals Dreams can also teach us to set big goals. If you want something to happen for real, like learning to fly a plane or invent a new ice cream flavor, dreams and imagination can push you to work hard. When we dream big, we can try to make those dreams real. This lets us live an exciting, adventurous life! Our dreams give us ideas for big goals we can reach. So dream big tonight, and dream big when you're awake too! Your awesome imagination is always there to use and explore.

Many people have achieved great things, be inspired by them.

When people dream big, they can end up in more fulfilling careers, relationships, or gaining strong skills by trying to achieve goals that first seemed impossible. Accomplishing aims that once felt out of reach can improve lives and provide a sense of achievement.

Those Who Dream Big Are Happier

People who aspire to big dreams tend to be happier as they constantly pursue happiness and success. Through perseverance, they build high self-esteem and can bounce back from failures by focusing on possibilities ahead. They feel excited about life and what it holds. They value their dreams and make efforts to attain them. When seemingly impossible dreams are achieved, like winning Olympic gold or publishing a book, people feel extremely happy and proud.

Dreams Are Free

You don't need any resources to simply dream. Everyone should start by dreaming before attempting to accomplish goals or be successful. Just having hopes and dreams opens up so many possibilities! If you keep working hard nothing can stop a dream becoming reality. Those without dreams often feel unfulfilled and empty. Imagining future goals gives people hope and without that they can feel hollow, like they are just drifting through life. Knowing what you want from the future eliminates uncertainty. The more you visualize dreams, the clearer your path ahead becomes.

Advice for Nurturing Big Dreams

1. Find inspiration in what others have achieved. All highly successful people started small before becoming "great". Reading their stories motivates and sparks fresh ideas. Imagine yourself facing their challenges and beating the odds, to set your sights even higher.

2. Keep a dream journal. Write down your dreams to remind yourself amidst the busyness of life. Having them visible keeps them top of mind.

3. Make a strategy. Simply dreaming is very different to making dreams reality. You need a plan to make them happen. As Scott Adams says, "Winners have systems, losers have goals." A good strategy allows for flexibility as dreams evolve.

4. Commit daily. Big dreams can feel overwhelming. But like eating an elephant, tackle them bit by bit each day. Small consistent steps lead to significant progress over time.

Why Your Aspirations Or Vision Are Crucial?

Developing a Vision

Having a bold vision for your future helps define where you want to go in life. This applies to both businesses and people.

Your big, vivid picture of how you desire your life to be is called your dream or vision. Even if you currently face setbacks, view them in context of your vision to keep perspective.

Consider Jesse's story. He had to get laid off before reassessing what he wanted. He realized auto parts weren't his dream career. His passion was being around finished, expensive vehicles.

When Jesse was let go last year, he felt his world collapse. Although he'd delivered auto parts since high school, he loved being around cars. But he'd never been promoted. Jesse now sells expensive sports cars at a dealership that values his expertise. As he says, "I've always wanted to work with vehicles. This sales role is perfect for me. I look forward to coming in each day."

When you believe in yourself, you support your true dreams. Chasing dreams helps you:

- Gain clarity on what you really want
- Feel motivated by having a purpose
- Build confidence as you progress

You Can Dream at Any Age

Age doesn't matter when chasing dreams. The key is to dream big then make those dreams reality.

9

Confidence Steps

When you are confident, this means you trust your abilities, skills, and judgement. Anyone who has a high self-confidence about themselves aren't afraid of making mistakes.

- Take on leadership roles
- Feel comfortable speaking up in groups
- Make friends more easily
- Manage stress better
- Reach goals and potential

Confidence grows when kids gain skills and knowledge. Feeling capable in one area like sports or music boosts overall self-assurance. Confidence leads to trying harder in school which leads to real achievement.

Tips for Parents and Teachers

Parents or teachers can finds this tips super helpful as they work towards making every teen become more confident:

- **Praise effort** - Compliment hard work and persistence. Don't just praise talent. This teaches kids that success comes from practiced skills.
- **Allow mistakes** - Correct gently and reframe mistakes as learning opportunities, not failures. This encourages risk-taking.
- **Track progress** - Note incremental improvements and achievements. This shows kids their abilities are developing.

- **Encourage interests** - Support activities the child enjoys. Mastery boosts confidence to try new challenges.
- **Ignore comparisons** - Don't compare students to peers or siblings. Help kids focus on being the best version of themselves.

Building real confidence is the key alongside verbal encouragement. Break larger goals into small, achievable steps. Guide students as they tackle increasingly difficult tasks. Scaffold the learning process while allowing independence.

Fun Confidence-Building Activities

Do you ever feel worried, shy, or not good enough? It's normal to feel this way sometimes. But there are lots of fun activities to help you see how special you are!

1. Draw a Self Portrait

You will need crayons, some markers to paint your drawings and a new picture of yourself . then start drawing a picture of you. Write on it these words "I am..." you can add other nice things people say about you. Look at your awesome portrait when you need a confidence boost!

2. Decorate a Confidence Box

Take a shoe box and cover the outside with pictures and words from magazines that show how others see you. Then fill the inside of the box with pictures, words and other things that show how you see yourself on the inside.

Share your box with someone you trust to talk about your strengths and how to gain even more confidence.

3. Start a Positivity Journal

Make a list of all your positive qualities - like being a good friend or athlete. Then each day, write down examples of times you showed those good qualities through your actions. Writing down the ways you shine wonderful!

Activity

4. Give Thanks

Make a gratitude journal to write down all the things big and small that you feel grateful for, like your family, teachers, friends or a sunny day. Studies show that focusing on what you feel lucky to have gives your mood and confidence a nice boost!

5. Note Positive Thoughts

Write down how having confidence helps you - like doing better on tests or making more friends more easily. Spend a week trying to think positive, uplifting thoughts about yourself. Jot down these thoughts on sticky notes and post them around your room. See how paying attention to your inner strengths makes you feel better about yourself!

6. Offer Advice

Pretend you have an advice column and write letters back to imaginary kids who struggle with confidence. Giving tips to boost their self-esteem will help you realize how many ideas you have to help yourself feel more sure of your own abilities.

7. Boost a Character

Imagine a story you have heard or read about. Cjhoose a shy fictional character from it and think about why such character lacked confidence. How do you think their life would have turned out if they had a high self confidence?

8. Set Self-Improvement Goals

Look closely at different parts of your life - like your use of social media or how you view your body. Choose 2 positive ways you can make little changes or set goals in each area to feel better about yourself overall. Remember that getting to know your needs helps you gain confidence.

9. Write Positive Affirmations

Fill out prompts like "I have a talent for..." and "I feel good about myself when..." with all the great things you know are wonderful about you! Seeing pages of positive traits, abilities, and accomplishments helps your self-esteem grow.

10. Get Active!

Research shows that exercising makes you feel better about yourself - especially if you play school or team sports. Ask about joining a fun activity like dance, martial arts or basketball. When you feel good physically, your confidence gets a boost too!

The most important tip is to focus on all your inner and outer positives. Confidence comes from believing in yourself and all you have to offer. Now get out there and feel great about the amazing person that you are!

Learning happens across settings, not just formally in school. Incorporate confidence-building during play:

- **Creative writing** - Have kids write short stories to accompany their drawings and artwork. This builds storytelling skills.

- **Club participation** - Organize groups centered around hobbies like coding or arts and crafts. Give each child a role and task.
- **Special roles** - Allow students opportunities like line leader, morning announcer, attendance taker. Rotate roles. Reinforce effort.
- **Presentations** - Ask children to present short speeches, skits, or show and tell on topics of interest. Use prompts, timers.
- **Team tasks** - Have kids work collaboratively on hands-on group projects like designing a zoo enclosure. Guide brainstorming and division of duties.
- **Goal setting** - Before exams, have students track past scores, identify weak areas, set improvement goals, make study plans. Review goals periodically.

Stories and Examples

Here are some real-world stories and examples showing confidence helping kids learn:

Maria's Story

Maria felt very shy about raising her hand and would only speak if called on. Her teacher reassured Maria that her insights were valuable. Maria was given a small solo part in the class play alongside some group singing roles. The experience helped Maria become more comfortable with public speaking. Now she volunteers answers, joins discussions, and is considering trying out for the school debate team next year!

Basketball Example

Andre loves basketball but would get frustrated and anxious before games worrying about making mistakes. His coach worked on techniques to manage performance anxiety. She taught deep breathing, positive self-talk strategies, and visualization of success. Andre would picture himself relaxed, focused and sinking baskets. Feeling more confident in his skills allowed Andre to play and enjoy himself during games.

Exercises to Boost Self-Esteem

Be ready to take action with these steps:

1. Positive Affirmations

2. Write uplifting statements about yourself e.g. "I am capable.

Note :

3. You can pen down the things you are grateful for each day.

4. Make a list of your strengths and best

qualities.

5. **Celebrate these unique strengths as part of your identity.**

6. Set realistic, achievable goals.

SETTING SMART GOALS

Instructions: Define a specific, measurable, achievable, relevant, and time-bound goal, break it down into actionable steps with assigned deadlines, anticipate obstacles and develop strategies to overcome them, track progress, seek accountability, and regularly review and adjust your goals.

S — **Specific**: What exactly do you want to achieve?

M — **Measurable**: How will you track your advancement?

A — **Attainable**: Evaluate the feasibility of your goal.

R — **Relevant**: How does it fit into your broader objectives?

T — **Time-bound**: What is the deadline?

7. Do random acts of kindness for others e.g. compliments or helping someone in need.
8. Make time for activities like relaxing baths, practicing mindfulness or enjoying hobbies.

Final Thoughts

The world needs your ideas and talents. You have power to positively impact others by pursuing dreams, despite fears.

We believe in the courage to dream big! Reach for the stars. You've got nothing to lose.

www.ingramcontent.com/pod-product-compliance
Lightning Source LLC
Chambersburg PA
CBHW051550010526
44118CB00022B/2645